Report from the Besieged City

REPORT FROM THE

BESIEGED CITY

& OTHER POEMS BY

ZBIGNIEW HERBERT

TRANSLATED WITH AN

INTRODUCTION & NOTES

BY JOHN CARPENTER

& BOGDANA CARPENTER

The Ecco Press / New York

Published by The Ecco Press in 1985
18 West 30th Street, New York, N.Y. 10001
Published simultaneously in Canada by Stoddart,
a subsidiary of General Publishing Co., Ltd., Don Mills
Printed in the United States of America
Library of Congress Cataloging in Publication Data
Herbert, Zbigniew.
  Report from the besieged city and other poems.
  Translation of: Raport z oblezonego miasta i inne wiersze
Includes bibliographical references.
I. Carpenter, John.   II. Carpenter, Bogdana.
III. Title.
PG7167.E64R313   1985   891.8'517   84–13634
ISBN 0–88001–71–1

FIRST EDITION

Some of these poems have appeared in Encounter,
The New York Times, Michigan Quarterly Review,
The Manhattan Review, The Malahat Review,
The Kenyon Review, Poetry Nation, Dissent, and Mr. Cogito.

Contents

Introduction by John Carpenter
and Bogdana Carpenter   vii

What I Saw   3
From the Top of the Stairs   4
Mr. Cogito's Soul   6
Lament   8
To the River   9
Old Masters   10
Prayer of Mr. Cogito—Traveler   12
Mr. Cogito—the Return   14
Mr. Cogito and the Imagination   17
In Memoriam Nagy László   20
To Ryszard Krynicki—a Letter   21
Mr. Cogito and Longevity   23
Mr. Cogito on Virtue   26
Shameful Dreams   28
Eschatological Forebodings of Mr. Cogito   29
Cradle Song   32
Photograph   34
Babylon   35
The Divine Claudius   36
The Monster of Mr. Cogito   39
The Murderers of Kings   43
Damastes (Also Known As Procrustes) Speaks   44
Anabasis   45
The Abandoned   46
Beethoven   49
Mr. Cogito Thinks About Blood   50
Mr. Cogito and Maria Rasputin—an Attempt at Contact   53
The Trial   58
Isadora Duncan   60
The Messenger   62
September 17   63
Mr. Cogito on the Need for Precision   64

The Power of Taste   69
Mr. Cogito—Notes from the House of the Dead   71
Report from the Besieged City   76

Translators' Notes   79

Introduction

Zbigniew Herbert is one of the finest poets now living in Europe. He has been translated into almost every European language, and has been awarded numerous prizes, among them the Jurzykowski Prize (1964), the Austrian Government Prize for European Literature (1965), and the Petrarch Prize (1979). During the last two years he has received other awards and honors in the West, but he has chosen to remain in Poland and not to negotiate with the authorities for a passport. Herbert has always resisted categorization—he has never been a spokesman for a group of any kind, and if he is a spokesman at all it is for the individual conscience. Completely alone, he nevertheless manages to pitch his voice in such a way that he is one of the most authentically public poets of our time:

> *for so many months years I was composing the final speech*
> *to God to the court of the world to the conscience*
> *to the dead rather than the living*
> > *—from "The Trial"*

Czesław Miłosz has written of Herbert, "If the key to contemporary Polish poetry is the collective experience of the last decades, Herbert is perhaps the most skilful in expressing it."[1] Yet his poetry is deliberately antirhetorical, and he lowers his voice rather than raising it, the rhythms of his poems sometimes approaching the level of a whisper, or silent thinking.

The present translation has been made from the author's typescript. Two small, limited editions of *Report from the Besieged City* have appeared in Poland. The first edition was published by internees in the Rakowiecka Prison in Warsaw in 1983. Almost all copies were confiscated. A second was published by Wydawnictwo Dobra Powszedniego in Warsaw in early 1984. A third edition of the Polish text was published in Paris at the end of 1983.[2] It is Herbert's sixth individual collection of poems; all thirty-five poems of the book are translated and included here. Herbert has also published two volumes of *Collected Poems* and two volumes of *Selected Poems* in Warsaw.

1. Czesław Miłosz, *Postwar Polish Poetry: An Anthology.* New York: Doubleday, 1965, p. 89.
2. Kultura (Maison Littéraire).

Like many Polish writers, Herbert comes from the East. He was born in 1924 in Lwów, which was then a cosmopolitan mix of Eastern European cultures, mostly Polish, Ukrainian, and Jewish. Herbert's mother was Armenian; his father was a lawyer and professor of economics. "Hence," Herbert has said, "my syncretic religion: Orthodox from my grandmother, Catholic by my father, and all around, evidences of Hassidic culture."[3] Herbert's un-Polish surname comes from another strain of his family; the father of Herbert's grandfather spoke only English, and came to Eastern Europe when the family divided into two branches, one Catholic and one Protestant. His great-uncle had been an Austrian general; this line of the family ended when Herbert's uncle, the general's son, received a Russian bullet in the back of his head in Katyn in 1940. On September 17, 1939, Lwów was invaded by the Soviet Union, in accordance with the protocols of the Molotov-Ribbentrop pact; for twenty months eastern Poland was in the hands of the Red Army and the N.K.V.D., until June 1941, when the Germans surprised their Soviet ally with an attack. The war did not end with the defeat of the Germans in 1945, when there was a brief, cruel civil war, followed by arrests, deportations, and executions of Home Army officers. Herbert managed to survive, doing odd jobs in Kraków, Toruń, Gdańsk, and Warsaw, and studying.

In 1946 in Poland and other European countries, many writers thought that prewar culture and its traditions had little relevance to what they had recently lived through. Past literary modes and styles were thought by many to be unsuitable to the new present; poetry was sometimes referred to between quotes, as if poets did not think of themselves as writing "poetry" at all but something quite different. The War Generation of writers in Poland is sometimes referred to as the Generation of "Kolumbowie" or Columbuses: it was they who first explored the new postwar social and political reality. Few assumptions about the world and civilization—about what it is, and what it is not—survived the war unscathed. Herbert's own doubts and experiments at this period were influenced by his studies in art, law, and above all philosophy. Herbert did not come to write poetry like a "philosopher" or use technical language; what was important, under the pressure of conflicting assertions and hard realities, was the desire to look closely and intently at the world, at ordinary objects or feelings, stripped of any bias.[4]

3. W. L. Webb in *The Guardian*, July 23, 1981.
4. Zbigniew Herbert, *Poezje wybrane*, Ludowa Spółdzielnia Wydawnicza, Warszawa, 1970, pp. 11–12.

The attempt to see clearly led to the question of language. How was their experience to be rendered by means of words, and syntax?

You understand [Herbert has written] *I had words in abundance to express my rebellion and protest. I might have written something of this sort: 'O you cursed, damned people, so-and-sos, you kill innocent people, wait and a just punishment will fall on you.' I didn't say this because I wanted to bestow a broader dimension on the specific, individual, experienced situation, or rather, to show its deeper, general human perspectives.*[5]

Many of Herbert's poems address the problem of how it is possible to describe the world, to "write" it, and he has approached the concern from a variety of angles. Like other contemporary poets, Herbert turned to the avant-garde in his quest for serviceable forms. In England and America, the traditional use of punctuation was maintained after the war as it had been used prior to it, with few exceptions; accepted practice was not put into doubt by new experience. But in Eastern Europe, especially countries that had been occupied and had experienced severe destruction, punctuation and other previously accepted practices—often formal—were sharply questioned. Punctuation had broad implications: what, for example, was its psychological basis? When we participate in an experience or action, does it present itself in a "punctuated" form, or is the punctuation only a result of posterior reflection—hence inorganic to the experience in its original form? Many of the experiments with forms and punctuation during this time were of a very serious nature. As Herbert writes in the poem "Mr. Cogito and the Imagination," he was never tempted by artificial fireworks or by "the piano at the top of the Alps." Throughout his career he has been faithful to directness, and to what he calls "uncertain clarity."

A number of poems in this collection have a very contemporary reference, and it is interesting to observe Herbert's use of metaphor in his quest for precision. Metaphor plays a very important functional role in his writings—the word suggests a transference of meaning away from a literal context, but for Herbert it does not serve impressionism, or divert the gaze focused intently on experience, on its meaning. Seemingly fanciful, the metaphors often serve to underline a salient or essential trait, they maintain and sharpen distinctions rather than obliterate them. For ex-

5. Ibid., p. 8.

ample, instead of naming an unimportant and soon-to-be-forgotten party leader, he speaks of a "dynastic fish" thrashing in a net. In "The Trial," the organization that has orchestrated the nightmarish proceedings is referred to as the party "of those without pity." For similar reasons he declines to give the names of his "watery-eyed gray foolish persecutors" —what he desires to avoid above all is "the babble of the speaker's platform the black foam of the newspapers."

The concern for the truth, for undistorted experience, also applies to the past. For Herbert the experience of the past is much like our own, and history is a fertile source of analogies. His use of the past is original and like that of no other writer alive. Historical figures and personae abound in his work; in sheer variety they recall those of Kierkegaard. In this volume their use is restrained, and the persona who recurs most frequently, "Mr. Cogito," is actually a pseudo-persona, a device permitting Herbert to make fun of himself (the "suckling Cogito") or to lighten an otherwise earnest enquiry. The other personae act and think in a broad historical continuum that is intensely present and alive. Herbert uses the past not as an escape from the present but as a means to focus attention on the present, to define it and its events.[6] For example, the poem "September 17" is topical; yet the poem evokes a broad range of history, and the title refers to an event not from recent years but to September 17, 1939—the date of the invasion of eastern Poland by the Soviet Union. The poem deals with not one but numerous comparable invasions. And the title poem, "Report from the Besieged City," refers not to a single siege but many, recurring, like the seasons, deep into the historical past. On the other hand, Damastes and Claudius are not simply destructive, utopian reformers from the ancient world; the two poems in which they appear clearly have a twentieth-century reference, and the analogies between them and more recent despots underline the psychological mechanisms involved: the mind that could conceive of death as "a runny nose," or that could imagine social reform in terms of cutting off the physical limbs of individuals.

A major theme of this new collection is the need to bear witness to the truth. Earlier poems have expressed this as a categorical imperative,[7] and *Report from the Besieged City* develops the theme further. Each individual must see events, and his own experience of them, clearly. No

6. See Bogdana Carpenter, "Zbigniew Herbert's Attack against Myth" in *Cross Currents. A Yearbook of Central European Culture.* 1984, Ann Arbor, Michigan.
7. Especially "The Envoy of Mr. Cogito" in Zbigniew Herbert, *Selected Poems,* Oxford–London–New York, 1977, pp. 79–80.

matter what obstacles are in his way, he must be faithful to the truth of this experience and keep a covenant with it. This covenant unites the individual to others, whether in the present or past, who have also struggled to see clearly and give expression to the truth. The greatest enemy to clarity is the manipulation of information, and of reality, at the service of power and propaganda—the "monster." The acquisition of truth is a constant battle; each person is surrounded by false information, and those who have access to the truth methodically withhold it—"those at the top of the stairs" rarely appear, and when they do it is with a hushing finger at the lips. The "Anonymous" author of the events on the stage of contemporary history hurriedly rings down a blood-drenched curtain to prevent the audience from seeing what has really taken place. The withholding of truth is a major strategy of power, the deliberate and concerted misrepresentation on the broadest scale, aiming ultimately at a forcible change of collective identity through the media, publishing, and political organs. Although this theme applies above all to the Communist world, it also has some application to the West, and the message gains in force, in universality, because of it.

In consequence, keeping this covenant has none of the ease, for example, of keeping a promise: it is an unequal and desperate struggle. Even direct experience is fallible. Witnesses can lose all sense of judgment due to excitement or fear; even the eyes deceive, leaving only touch—the most concrete of the senses—that gives the most reliable evidence of truth and is closest to the reality of experience. The link forged by Herbert between the truth of concrete, lived experience on the one hand and precision on the other is one of the most original features of his work:

> *accuracy is essential*
> *we must not be wrong*
> *even by a single one*
>
> *we are despite everything*
> *the guardians of our brothers*

> —*from "Mr. Cogito on the Need for Precision"*

Another important theme of this collection is suffering, and its relation to revolt. Suffering, also, is close to the sense of touch and a verification of experience. The main value of suffering is that, passing by way of compassion, it leads to revolt. There is no cultivation of suffering for its own sake: the notion of redemption through passive acceptance of suffer-

[xi

ing is totally foreign to Herbert. Poems like "Notes from the House of the Dead," "Babylon," and "Report from the Besieged City" depict suffering in an open-eyed, clear manner, without illusions. Revolt does not lead to immediate victory against sheer naked force and repression, yet the revolt foresees this and continues, for the covenant—and legitimacy—are not on the side of physical power but of the rebellion against it. Resistance makes use of suffering, and the memory of it, in trying to overcome it. Suffering must be kept alive for freedom to have real meaning because it is not an automatic inheritance—it is easily forfeited by complacency, as in the poem "Babylon," and becomes overgrown with grass: by lack of memory, passivity, and defeat. The "City" must be kept alive by the individual within his own mind, without counting on support from others, and in the face of betrayal; in doing this the individual becomes what he defends, and he becomes the City wherever he is.

Resistance—*opór, résistance, motstand*—became a strong tradition in many European countries invaded and occupied by German armies during World War II. In contemporary Poland, Herbert is taking this theme and developing it even further. Our own freedom and our very reality depend upon the accuracy with which we are able to perceive the suffering around us, to bear witness to it, and to revolt against it. In opposition to an apparatus that has concentrated power and the control of information to a degree not seen before, rarely has the theme of individual revolt been expressed with such force.

John Carpenter
Bogdana Carpenter

Ann Arbor, Michigan, 1984

Report from the Besieged City

What I Saw

To the memory of Kazimierz Moczarski

I saw prophets tearing at their pasted-on beards
I saw impostors joining sects of flagellants
butchers disguised in sheepskin
who fled the anger of the people
playing on a block-flute

I saw I saw

      I saw a man who had been tortured
      he now sat safely in the family circle
      cracked jokes ate soup
      I looked at the opened mouth
      his gums—two bramble twigs stripped of bark
      I saw his whole nakedness
      the whole humiliation

      later
      a solemn meeting
      many people flowers
      stifling
      someone spoke incessantly about deviations
      I thought of his deviated mouth

is this the last act
of the play by Anonymous
flat as a shroud
full of suppressed sobbing
and the snickering of those
who heave a sigh of relief
that again it has worked out
and after clearing away the dead props
slowly
raise

the blood-drenched curtain

               (1956)

From the Top of the Stairs

Of course
those who are standing at the top of the stairs
know
they know everything

with us it's different
sweepers of squares
hostages of a better future
those at the top of the stairs
appear to us rarely
with a hushing finger always at the mouth

we are patient
our wives darn the sunday shirts
we talk of food rations
soccer prices of shoes
while on saturday we tilt the head backward
and drink

we aren't those
who clench their fists
brandish chains
talk and ask questions
in a fever of excitement
urging to rebel
incessantly talking and asking questions

here is their fairy tale—
we will dash at the stairs
and capture them by storm
the heads of those who were standing at the top
will roll down the stairs
and at last we will gaze
at what can be seen from those heights
what future
what emptiness

[4

we don't desire the view
of rolling heads
we know how easily heads grow back
and at the top there will always remain
one or three
while at the bottom it is black from brooms and shovels

sometimes we dream
those at the top of the stairs
come down
that is to us
and as we are chewing bread over the newspaper
they say

      —now let's talk
         man to man
         what the posters shout out isn't true
         we carry the truth in tightly locked lips
         it is cruel and much too heavy
         so we bear the burden by ourselves
         we aren't happy
         we would gladly stay
         here

these are dreams of course
they can come true
or not come true
so we will
continue to cultivate
our square of dirt
square of stone

with a light head
a cigarette behind the ear
and not a drop of hope in the heart

                        (1956)

Mr. Cogito's Soul

In the past
we know from history
she would go out from the body
when the heart stopped

with the last breath
she went quietly away
to the blue meadows of heaven

      Mr. Cogito's soul
      acts differently

      during his life she leaves his body
      without a word of farewell

      for months for years she lives
      on different continents
      beyond the frontiers
      of Mr. Cogito

      it is hard to locate her address
      she sends no news of herself
      avoids contacts
      doesn't write letters

      no one knows when she will return
      perhaps she has left forever

Mr. Cogito struggles to overcome
the base feeling of jealousy

he thinks well of his soul
thinks of her with tenderness

undoubtedly she must live also
in the bodies of others

certainly there are too few souls
for all humanity

Mr. Cogito accepts his fate
he has no other way out

he even attempts to say
—my own soul mine

he thinks of his soul affectionately
he thinks of his soul with tenderness

therefore when she appears
unexpectedly
he doesn't welcome her with the words
—it's good you've come back

he only looks at her from an angle
as she sits before the mirror
combing her hair
tangled and gray

Lament

To the memory of my mother

And now she has over her head brown clouds of roots
a slim lily of salt on the temples beads of sand
while she sails on the bottom of a boat through foaming nebulas

a mile beyond us where the river turns
visible-invisible as the light on a wave
truly she isn't different—abandoned like all of us

To the River

River—hourglass of water metaphor of eternity
I enter you more and more changed
so I could be a cloud a fish or rock
while you are the same like a clock that measures
the metamorphoses of the body and descents of the spirit
slow disintegration of tissues and love

I who am born of clay
want to be your pupil
and learn the spring the Olympian heart
o cool torch rustling column
bedrock of my faith and my despair

river teach me stubbornness and endurance
so in the last hour I become worthy
of rest in the shade of the great delta
in the holy triangle of the beginning and of the end

Old Masters

The Old Masters
went without names

their signature
was the white fingers of the Madonna

or pink towers
di città sul mare

also scenes from the life
della Beatà Umiltà

they dissolved
in sogno
miràcolo
crocefissióne

they found shelter
under the eyelids of angels
behind hills of clouds
in the thick grass of paradise

they drowned without a trace
in golden firmaments
with no cry of fright
or call to be remembered

the surfaces of their paintings
are smooth as a mirror
they aren't mirrors for us
they are mirrors for the chosen

> I call on you Old Masters
> in hard moments of doubt
>
> make the serpent's scales of pride
> fall from me

let me be deaf
to the temptation of fame

I call upon you Old Masters

the Painter of the Rain of Manna
the Painter of Embroidered Trees
the Painter of the Visitation
the Painter of the Sacred Blood

Prayer of Mr. Cogito—Traveler

Lord
> I thank You for creating the world beautiful and very diverse

> also for permitting me in Your inexhaustible goodness to be in places
> that were not the places of my everyday torment
>> and
> —that at night in Tarquinia I lay down in a square near a well and
> the swinging bronze from a tower announced Your wrath or for-
> giveness

>> while a small donkey on the island of Corfu sang to me from his
>> incredible bellows lungs the melancholy of the landscape

>> and in the ugly city of Manchester I discovered people who were
>> sensible and good

>> nature repeated its wise tautologies: a forest was a forest the sea
>> was the sea rock was rock

>> stars moved in circles and it was as it should be—Jovis omnia
>> plena

> —forgive me that I thought only of myself when the lives of others
> turned circled around me cruelly irreversible like the great astro-
> logical clock of Saint Peter's in Beauvais

>> that I was lazy absent-minded too careful in labyrinths and grottos

>> forgive me also that I didn't fight like Lord Byron for the happi-
>> ness of captive peoples that I watched only risings of the moon
>> and museums

> —thank You that the works created for Your glory let me share a
> particle of their secret and I imagined in my great presumptuous-
> ness that Duccio Van Eyck Bellini painted also for me

and also the Acropolis which to the end I never understood patiently laying bare before me its mutilated body

—I ask You to reward the ancient white-haired man who brought me fruit from his garden without being asked on the burnt island where the son of Laertes was born

as well as Miss Helen on the misty island of Mull in the Hebrides who received me in a Greek manner and asked me to leave a lit lamp by the window at night facing holy Iona so the land's lights could greet each other

also all those who showed me the road and said kato kyrie kato

and take under your protection Mama of Spoleto Spiridion of Paxos the good student from Berlin who saved me in a difficult moment then unexpectedly met me in Arizona and drove me to the Grand Canyon which is like a hundred thousand cathedrals with their heads turned downward

—permit me O Lord not to think about my watery-eyed gray foolish persecutors when the sun sinks into the Ionian Sea truly indescribable

permit that I understand other people other tongues other sufferings

and above all else that I be humble which means he who desires the spring

thank You Lord for creating the world beautiful and diverse

and if it is Your seduction I am seduced forever and with no forgiveness

Mr. Cogito—the Return

1

Mr. Cogito
has made up his mind to return
to the stony bosom
of his homeland

the decision is dramatic
he will regret it bitterly

but no longer can he endure
empty everyday expressions
—comment allez-vous
—wie geht's
—how are you

at first glance simple the questions
demand a complicated answer

Mr. Cogito tears off
the bandages of polite indifference

he has stopped believing in progress
he is concerned about his own wound

displays of abundance
fill him with boredom

he became attached only
to a Dorian column
the Church of San Clemente
the portrait of a certain lady
a book he didn't have time to read
and a few other trifles

therefore he returns

he sees already
the frontier
a plowed field
murderous shooting towers
dense thickets of wire

soundless
armor-plated doors
slowly close behind him

and already
he is
alone
in the treasure-house
of all misfortunes

    2

so why does he return
ask friends
from the better world

he could stay here
somehow make ends meet

entrust the wound
to chemical stain-remover

leave it behind in waiting-rooms
of immense airports

so why is he returning

—to the water of childhood
—to entangled roots
—to the clasp of memory
—to the hand the face
seared on the grill of time

at first glance simple the questions
demand a complicated answer

probably Mr. Cogito returns
to give a reply

to the whisperings of fear
to impossible happiness
to the blow given from behind
to the deadly question

Mr. Cogito and the Imagination

1

Mr. Cogito never trusted
tricks of the imagination

the piano at the top of the Alps
played false concerts for him

he didn't appreciate labyrinths
the Sphinx filled him with loathing

he lived in a house with no basement
without mirrors or dialectics

jungles of tangled images
were not his home

he would rarely soar
on the wings of a metaphor
and then he fell like Icarus
into the embrace of the Great Mother

he adored tautologies
explanations
idem per idem

that a bird is a bird
slavery means slavery
a knife is a knife
death remains death

he loved
the flat horizon
a straight line
the gravity of the earth

2

Mr. Cogito will be numbered
among the species *minores*

he will accept indifferently the verdict
of future scholars of the letter

he used the imagination
for entirely different purposes

he wanted to make it
an instrument of compassion

he wanted to understand to the very end

—Pascal's night
—the nature of a diamond
—the melancholy of the prophets
—Achilles' wrath
—the madness of those who kill
—the dreams of Mary Stuart
—Neanderthal fear
—the despair of the last Aztecs
—Nietzsche's long death throes
—the joy of the painter of Lascaux
—the rise and fall of an oak
—the rise and fall of Rome

and so to bring the dead back to life
to preserve the covenant

Mr. Cogito's imagination
has the motion of a pendulum

it crosses with precision
from suffering to suffering

there is no place in it
for the artificial fires of poetry

he would like to remain faithful
to uncertain clarity

In Memoriam Nagy László

Romana said you had just left
which is how we usually speak of those who remain forever
I envy you your face of marble

between us matters were pure no letter
memories nothing entertaining the eye
no ring jug
or woman's lament
this is why it is easier to believe in a sudden elevation
that you are now like Attila Jozef
Mickiewicz Lord Byron beautiful phantoms
who always come to an appointed meeting

my sense of touch could not become tamed
rapacious love of the concrete demanded victims
we did not fill the dead chamber with our laughter
didn't rest our elbows against the rustling oak of a table
didn't drink wine or share a fate
yet we lived together
in the hospice of the Cross and Rose

the space that divides us is like a shroud
evening fog rises it falls
those who are noble have a face of water and earth

our further coexistence will probably follow
a geometrical law—two parallel lines
unearthly patience and inhuman faithfulness

To Ryszard Krynicki—a Letter

Not much will remain Ryszard really not much
of the poetry of this insane century certainly Rilke Eliot
a few other distinguished shamans who knew the secret
of conjuring a form with words that resists the action of time without which
no phrase is worth remembering and speech is like sand

those school notebooks of ours sincerely tormented
with traces of sweat tears blood will be
like the text of a song without music for the eternal proofreader
honorably righteous more than obvious

too easily we came to believe beauty does not save
that it leads the lighthearted from dream to dream to death
none of us knew how to awaken the dryad of a poplar
to read the writing of clouds
this is why the unicorn will not cross our tracks
we won't bring to life a ship in the bay a peacock a rose
only nakedness remained for us and we stand naked
on the right the better side of the triptych
the Last Judgment

we took public affairs on our thin shoulders
recording suffering the struggle with tyranny with lying
but—you have to admit—we had opponents despicably small
so was it worth it to lower holy speech
to the babble of the speaker's platform the black foam of the newspapers

in our poems Ryszard there is so little joy—daughter of the gods
too few luminous dusks mirrors wreaths of rapture
nothing but dark psalmodies stammering of animulae
urns of ashes in the burned garden

> in spite of fate the verdicts of history human misdeeds
> what strength is needed to whisper
> in the garden of betrayal—a silent night

what strength of spirit is needed to strike
beating blindly with despair against despair
a spark of light word of reconciliation

so the dancing circle will last forever on the thick grass
so the birth of a child and every beginning is blessed
gifts of air earth and fire and water

this I don't know—my friend—and is why
I am sending you these owl's puzzles in the night
a warm embrace
                    greetings from my shadow

Mr. Cogito and Longevity

1

Mr. Cogito
can be proud of himself

he has crossed the frontier of the life
of many other animals

> when a worker bee
> retires to eternal rest
> the suckling Cogito
> was enjoying exquisite health

> when cruel death
> takes away the house mouse
> he successfully recovered from whooping cough
> found speech and fire

> if we are to believe
> the theologists of birds
> the swallow's soul
> flies to paradise
> after ten
> terrestrial springs

> at this age
> young Master Cogito
> was studying the fourth grade
> of elementary school with varying success
> and began to take an interest in women

> then
> he won the Second World War
> (a doubtful victory)
> at the exact time when a goat
> wanders off to the Valhalla of goats

he performed no mean achievement
despite a few dictators
crossing the Rubicon of the half-century
bloody
but alive

he won
over the carp
the alligator
the crab

now he finds himself
between the final moment
of an eel
and the final moment
of an elephant

here
to speak truthfully
the ambitions of Mr. Cogito
come to an end

2

a coffin shared with an elephant
does not frighten him at all

he doesn't hunger for longevity
like the parrot
or Hippoglassus vulgaris

also
the soaring eagle
armor-plated turtle
silly swan

to the end
Mr. Cogito would like to sing
the beauty of the passage of time

this is why he doesn't gulp down Gelée Royale
or drink elixirs
doesn't make a pact with Mephisto

with the care of a good gardener
he cultivates the wrinkles on his face

humbly accepts calcium
deposited in his veins

he is delighted by lapses of memory
he was tormented by memory

immortality
since childhood
put him in a state
of trembling fear

      why should the gods be envied?

      —for celestial drafts
      —for a botched administration
      —for unsatiated lust

      —for a tremendous yawn

Mr. Cogito on Virtue

1

It is not at all strange
she isn't the bride
of real men

of generals
athletes of power
despots

through the ages she follows them
this tearful old maid
in a dreadful hat from the Salvation Army
she reprimands them

she drags out of the junkroom
a portrait of Socrates
a little cross molded from bread
old words

—while marvelous life reverberates all around
  ruddy as a slaughterhouse at dawn

she could almost be buried
in a silver casket
of innocent souvenirs

she becomes smaller and smaller
like a hair in the throat
like a buzzing in the ear

2

my God
if she was a little younger
a little prettier

kept up with the spirit of the times
swayed her hips
to the rhythm of popular music

maybe then she would be loved
by real men
generals athletes of power despots

if she took care of herself
looked presentable
like Liz Taylor
or the Goddess of Victory

but an odor of mothballs
wafts from her
she compresses her lips
repeats a great—No

unbearable in her stubbornness
ridiculous as a scarecrow
as the dream of an anarchist
as the lives of the saints

Shameful Dreams

Metamorphoses downward to the sources of history
the lost paradise of childhood in a drop of water

escapes chases through corridors of mice
an insect's travels to the bottom of a flower
a sharp awakening in an oriole's nest

or loping watchfully over the snow in a wolf's hide
and at the edge of an abyss a huge howling to the full moon
sudden fear when the wind brings the scent of a murderer

the whole sun setting in a stag's antlers
spiral dream of a snake
vertical alertness of the flatfish

all of them are recorded in the atlas of our body
and incised in the rock of the skull like portraits of our ancestors
so we repeat letters of forgotten speech

we dance at night before statues of animals
dressed in skin scales feathers and plated armor
infinite is the litany of our crimes

don't push us away good spirits
we have blundered on the oceans and stars too long
we are exhausted beyond measure accept us to the herd

Eschatological Forebodings of Mr. Cogito

1

So many miracles
in the life of Mr. Cogito
so many caprices of fortune
enchantments and falls
eternity therefore will probably
be bitter for him

without travel
friends
books

instead
time in abundance
like a patient with sick lungs
like an emperor in exile

probably he will sweep
the great square of Purgatory
or stand bored in front of the mirror
of an abandoned barber shop

without a pen
ink
parchment

with no memories of childhood
or universal history
atlas of birds

like the others
he will attend
courses on the eradication
of earthly habits

the recruiting commission
works very precisely

roots out vestiges of the senses
of candidates for paradise

Mr. Cogito will defend himself
he will put up a fierce resistance

   2

most willingly he will give up the sense of smell
he used it with moderation
never followed the tracks of anyone

also he will give away without regret
the taste of food
taste of hunger

on the table of the recruiting commission
he will surrender the petals of his ears

in his terrestrial life
he was a lover of the music of silence

he will only
explain to the severe angels

that the sense of sight and of touch
don't want to leave him

that he continues to feel in his body
all the earthly thorns
splinters
caresses
flame
whips of the sea

that still he continues to see
a pine on a mountain slope

dawn's seven candlesticks
a blue-veined stone

he will yield to all tortures
gentle persuasions
but to the end he will defend
the magnificent sensation of pain

and a few weathered images
on the bottom of the burned-out eye

3

who knows
perhaps he will manage
to convince the angels
he is incapable
of heavenly
service

and they will permit him to return
by an overgrown path
at the shore of a white sea
to the cave of the beginning

Cradle Song

The years shorter and shorter
                              priests at the temple of Ammon
discovered a Perpetually Burning Lamp uses less oil each year
which means the world is shrinking
                              space time and people

The priests' observation was handed down by Plutarch
provoking angry grumbling in circles of philosophers
who despaired at human changeability
and wanted the cosmos to shine for us as a model

Seemingly absurd the proof of the lamp
agrees with the experience of those who have left behind
inns stations houses crossed the torrent of illusions
and go now on the gentle slope where we all go

They know
          —days and nights diminish

          —a rose picked at dawn sheds petals in panic
            by evening it is only a burnt grove of stamens

          —between drowsiness in December and an August nap
            only a single moment passes without events and nostalgia

          —always fewer letters travels surprises

          —a candle slim as a needle in trembling fingers
            shows the way from one wall to another wall
            frozen mirrors refuse comfort

          —the precious dead numerous as banks of sand that look like sand
            the lodgings in our memory don't accept anyone

          —dust has settled in empty rooms and writes its memoirs

—the city of our birth fades and even the Ca d'Oro
no longer shines as all the places we have loved
sink into the sea on unstable lagoons

The Perpetually Burning Lamp uses less oil each year

This is how the good-hearted universe tucks us in to sleep

Photograph

This boy motionless as an arrow of Eleata
a boy amidst high grass has nothing in common with me
except a date of birth the papillary line

my father took this picture before the second Persian war
from the clouds and foliage I conclude it was August
the birds the crickets rang the smell of corn smell of a full moon

below the river called Hipanis on Roman maps
a watershed and nearby thunder advising them to take shelter with the
    Greeks
their colonies on the sea weren't too far

the boy smiles trustingly the only shadow he knows
is the shadow of a straw hat shadow of a pine tree shadow of the house
and if there is a glow it is the glow of sunset

      little one my Isaac bend your head
      it is only an instant of pain then you will be
      whatever you want—a swallow lily of the field

      so I must shed your blood my little one
      for you to remain innocent in the summer lightning
      safe for ever like an insect in amber
      beautiful as a cathedral of fern preserved in coal

Babylon

Years later when I returned to Babylon everything was changed
girls I had loved numbers of metro lines
I waited at the telephone sirens were stubbornly silent

so consolation by art—Petrus Christus the portrait of a young lady
became more and more flat folded its wings to sleep
lights of annihilation and of the city approached each other

the festival of the Apocalypse torches the false Sybil
absolved drunken crowds of worshipers of abundance
the trampled body of God was dragged in triumph and dust

this is the end of the world fully laden Etruscan tables
they are celebrating unaware of fate shirts stained with wine
in the end the barbarians come to slash the aorta

    city I didn't wish your death anyway not like this
    because the sweet fruit of freedom will go with you underground
    and everything must begin with bitter knowledge with grass

The Divine Claudius

It was said
I was begotten by Nature
but unfinished
like an abandoned sculpture
a sketch
the damaged fragment of a poem

for years I played the half-wit
idiots live more safely
I calmly put up with insults
if I planted all the pits
thrown into my face
an olive grove would spring up
a vast oasis of palms

I received a many-sided education
Livy the rhetoricians philosophers
I spoke Greek like an Athenian
although Plato I recalled
only in the lying position

I completed my studies
in dock-side taverns and brothels
those unwritten dictionaries of vulgar Latin
bottomless treasuries of crime and lust

after the murder of Caligula
I hid behind a curtain
they dragged me out by force
I didn't manage to adopt an intelligent expression
when they threw at my feet the world
ridiculous and flat

from then on I became the most diligent
emperor in universal history
a Hercules of bureaucracy
I recall with pride

my liberal law
giving permission to let out
sounds of the belly during feasts

I deny the charge of cruelty often made against me
in reality I was only absent-minded

on the day of Messalina's violent murder—
the poor thing was killed I admit on my orders—
I asked during the banquet—Why hasn't Madame come
a deathly silence answered me
really I forgot

sometimes it would happen I invited
the dead to a game of dice
I punished failure to attend with a fine
overburdened by so many labors
I might have made mistakes in details

it seems
I ordered thirty-five senators
and the cavalrymen of some three centurions
to be executed
well what of it
a bit less purple
fewer gold rings
on the other hand—and this isn't a trifle—
more room in the theater

no one wanted to understand
that the goal of these operations was sublime
I longed to make death familiar to people
to dull its edge
bring it down to the banal everyday dimension
of a slight depression or runny nose

and here is the proof
of my delicacy of feeling
I removed the statue of gentle Augustus
from the square of executions

so the sensitive marble
wouldn't hear the roars of the condemned

my nights were devoted to study
I wrote the history of the Etruscans
a history of Carthage
a bagatelle about Saturn
a contribution to the theory of games
and a treatise on the venom of serpents

it was I who saved Ostia
from the invasion of sand
I drained swamps
built aqueducts
since then it has become easier
in Rome to wash away blood

I expanded the frontiers of the empire
by Brittany Mauretania
and if I recall correctly Thrace

my death was caused by my wife Agrippina
and an uncontrollable passion for boletus
mushrooms—the essence of the forest—became the essence of death

descendants—remember with proper respect and honor
at least one merit of the divine Claudius
I added new signs and sounds to our alphabet
expanded the limits of speech that is the limits of freedom

the letters I discovered—beloved daughters—Digamma and Antisigma
led my shadow
as I pursued the path with tottering steps to the dark land of Orkus

The Monster of Mr. Cogito

1

Lucky Saint George
from his knight's saddle
could exactly evaluate
the strength and movements of the dragon

the first principle of strategy
is to assess the enemy accurately

Mr. Cogito
is in a worse position

he sits in the low
saddle of a valley
covered with thick fog

through fog it is impossible to perceive
fiery eyes
greedy claws
jaws

through fog
one sees only
the shimmering of nothingness

the monster of Mr. Cogito
has no measurements

it is difficult to describe
escapes definition

it is like an immense depression
spread out over the country

it can't be pierced
with a pen

with an argument
or spear

were it not for its suffocating weight
and the death it sends down
one would think
it is the hallucination
of a sick imagination

but it exists
for certain it exists

like carbon monoxide it fills
houses temples markets

poisons wells
destroys the structures of the mind
covers bread with mold

the proof of the existence of the monster
is its victims

it is not direct proof
but sufficient

2

reasonable people say
we can live together
with the monster

we only have to avoid
sudden movements
sudden speech

if there is a threat
assume the form
of a rock or a leaf

listen to wise Nature
recommending mimicry

that we breathe shallowly
pretend we aren't there

    Mr. Cogito however
    does not want a life of make-believe

    he would like to fight
    with the monster
    on firm ground

    so he walks out at dawn
    into a sleepy suburb
    carefully equipped
    with a long sharp object

    he calls to the monster
    on the empty streets

    he offends the monster
    provokes the monster

    like a bold skirmisher
    of an army that doesn't exist

    he calls—
    come out contemptible coward

    through the fog
    one sees only
    the huge snout of nothingness

        Mr. Cogito wants to enter
        the uneven battle

        it ought to happen
        possibly soon

before there will be
a fall from inertia
an ordinary death without glory
suffocation from formlessness

The Murderers of Kings

As Regis asserts they resemble one another
like twins Ravaillac and Princip Clément and Caserio
often they come from families of epileptics and suicides
they however are healthy that is ordinary
usually young very young and so they remain for eternity

their solitude for months years they sharpen their knives
and in the woods outside town conscientiously learn how to shoot
they work out the assassination are alone painstaking and very honest
they give the pennies they earn to their mothers take care of their brothers
    and sisters don't drink
have no friends or girls

                  after the coup they give themselves up without
                        resistance
bear tortures bravely don't ask for clemency
reject any accomplices suggested during the investigation
there wasn't a conspiracy truly they were alone

                  their inhuman sincerity and simplicity
irritates the judges the defense the public greedy for sensation

                those who send souls
to the beyond are amazed at the calm of the condemned in their final hour

calm lack of anger regret or even hatred
almost radiance

                so their brains are ransacked
the heart weighed liver cut however no departure
from the norm is discovered

not one of them managed to change the course of history
but the dark message has gone from generation to generation
so these small hands are worthy of reflection
small hands in which the certainty of the blow is trembling

Damastes (Also Known As Procrustes) Speaks

My movable empire between Athens and Megara
I ruled alone over forests ravines precipices
without the advice of old men foolish insignia with a simple club
dressed only in the shadow of a wolf
and terror caused by the sound of the word Damastes

I lacked subjects that is I had them briefly
they didn't live as long as dawn however it is slander
to say I was a bandit as the falsifiers of history claim

in reality I was a scholar and social reformer
my real passion was anthropometry

I invented a bed with the measurements of a perfect man
I compared the travelers I caught with this bed
it was hard to avoid—I admit—stretching limbs cutting legs
the patients died but the more there were who perished
the more I was certain my research was right
the goal was noble progress demands victims

I longed to abolish the difference between the high and the low
I wanted to give a single form to disgustingly varied humanity
I never stopped in my efforts to make people equal

my life was taken by Theseus the murderer of the innocent Minotaur
the one who went through the labyrinth with a woman's ball of yarn
an impostor full of tricks without principles or a vision of the future

I have the well-grounded hope others will continue my labor
and bring the task so boldly begun to its end

Anabasis

The condottieri of Cyrus a foreign legion
cunning pitiless and yes they killed
two hundred and fifteen daily marches
—kill us we can't go any further—
thirty-four thousand two hundred and fifty-five stadia

festering with sleeplessness they went through savage countries
uncertain fords mountain passes in snow and salty plateaus
cutting their road in the living body of peoples
luckily they didn't lie they were defending civilization

the famous shout on Mount Teches
is mistakenly interpreted by sentimental poets
they simply found the sea that is the exit from the dungeon

they made the journey without the Bible without prophets burning bushes
without signs on the earth without signs in the sky
with the cruel consciousness that life is immense

The Abandoned

1

I did not catch
the last transport

I stayed behind in a town
that is not a town

without morning
or evening newspapers

it doesn't have
prisons
clocks
water

I enjoy
great vacations
outside of time

I go for long walks
through avenues of burned houses
avenues of sugar
of broken glass
of rice

I could write a treatise
on the sudden transformation
of life into archeology

2

there is a huge silence

the artillery in the suburbs
has choked on its own courage

sometimes
all that can be heard
is the bell of collapsing walls

and the light thunder
of sheet metal dangling in the air

there is a huge silence
before the night of the predators

at times
an absurd airplane
appears in the sky

it drops leaflets
calling for surrender

I would do it willingly
but there is no one to surrender to

3

I live now
in the best hotel

the dead porter
remains on duty in his room

from a hill of rubble
I enter directly
onto the second floor
to the suite
of the former mistress
of the former chief of police

I sleep on sheets of newspapers
I cover myself with a poster
announcing the final victory

in the bar there is still
medicine for solitude

bottles with yellow fluid
and a symbolic label

—Johnnie
    tipping his top hat
    walking rapidly toward the West

I have no resentment against anyone
that I was abandoned

I was short
of luck
and the right hand

on the ceiling
a light bulb
recalls a skull turned upside down

I wait for the victors

I drink to the fallen
I drink to the deserters

I overcame
bad thoughts

I was abandoned even
by the presentiment of death

Beethoven

They say he became deaf—but it isn't true
the demons of his hearing worked tirelessly
and the dead lake never slept in the shells of his ears

otitis media then acuta
brought into the hearing mechanism
squeaky tones hisses

a hollow sound whistle of a thrush wooden bell of the forest
he took from it as well as he could—a high descant of violins
undergrown by the deep blackness of basses

the list of his illnesses passions failures
is as rich as the catalogue of completed works
tympano-labyrinthine sclerosis probably syphilis

finally what had to come came—immense stupor
mute hands thrashing dark boxes and strings
the puffed-out cheeks of angels acclaiming silence

typhus in childhood later angina pectoris arteriosclerosis
in the Cavatine quartet opus 130
you can hear shallow panting the compressed heart suffocation

messy quarrelsome with a pockmarked face
he drank beyond measure and cheaply—beer coachman's schnapps
weakened by tuberculosis the liver refused to play

> there is nothing to regret—the creditors died
> the mistresses cooks and countesses also died
> princes protectors—the candelabra sobbed

> as if he were still living he borrows money scrambles
> between heaven and earth to make contacts

> but the moon is the moon even without the sonata

Mr. Cogito Thinks About Blood

1

Reading a book
on the horizons of science
the history of the progress of thought
from the murk of faith
to the light of knowledge
Mr. Cogito came upon an episode
that has darkened
his private horizon
with a cloud

a tiny contribution
to the obese history
of fatal human errors

for a long time
the conviction persisted
man carries in himself
a sizable reservoir of blood

a squat barrel
twenty-odd liters
—a trifle

from this we can understand
the effusive descriptions of battles
fields red as coral

gushing torrents of gore
a sky that repeats
infamous hecatombs

and also the universal
method of cure

the artery
of a sick man was opened
and the precious liquid
let lightheartedly out
into a tin basin

not everyone lived through it
Descartes whispered in agony
Messieurs épargnez—

2

now we know exactly
that in the body of each man
the condemned and the executioner
scarcely flows
four to five liters
of what used to be called
the body's soul

a few bottles of Burgundy
a pitcher
one-fourth
of the capacity of a pail

very little

Mr. Cogito
is naively astonished
this discovery
did not create a revolution
in the domain of customs

at least it should incline
people to reasonable thrift

we may not
wastefully squander as before
on battlefields
on places of execution

really there isn't much of it
less than water oil
our resources of energy

but it happened otherwise
shameful conclusions were drawn

instead of restraint
wastefulness

the precise measurement
strengthened nihilists
gave a greater impetus to tyrants
now they know exactly
that man is fragile
and it is easy to drain him of blood

four to five liters
an amount without significance

therefore the triumph of science
did not bring substance for thought
a principle of behavior
a moral norm

it is small consolation
thinks Mr. Cogito
that the exertions of scientists
have not changed the course of affairs

they hardly weigh as much
as the sigh of a poet

and the blood
continues to flow

goes beyond the horizons of the body
the limits of fantasy

—probably there will be a deluge

Mr. Cogito and Maria Rasputin— an Attempt at Contact

1

Sunday
early afternoon
sweltering heat

in distant California
years ago—

> leafing through
> *The Voice of the Pacific*
> Mr. Cogito
> is informed
> of the death of Maria Rasputin
> daughter of Rasputin the Terrible
>
> a brief note
> on the last page
> touched him personally
> deeply moved him
>
> and yet nothing
> linked him to Maria
> whose meager life
> cannot be unwound
> into the carpet of a poem
>
> here is the outline of her story
> in a few strokes
> and somewhat trivial:

> > at that time
> > when the usurper Vladimir Ilych
> > exterminated the anointed Nicolas
> > Maria took shelter
> > on the other side of the ocean

she exchanged willows
for palm trees

served
at the homes of white émigrés
in an aroma of native speech
of blini cucumbers borscht

she had the strange ambition
to wash the plates
of the well-born

if not a prince
then at least a baron
in the last resort a widow
of an officer in the bodyguard

unexpectedly
the doors to an artistic career
opened before her

she made her debut
in a silent film
The Jolly Sailor Jimmie

the miserable picture
did not secure for Maria
a permanent place
in the history of the Tenth Muse

later
she appeared in variety shows
second-rate music halls
cabarets

finally
her apotheosis

she won fame
for an act in a circus
A Dance with the Bear
or Siberian Wedding

the sensation lasted briefly
her partner Misha
seized her too passionately
the violent caress
of her abandoned homeland

by a miracle she came out of it alive

that's all
plus
two unsuccessful marriages

and one more important detail

she proudly rejected an offer
to publish a fictitious autobiography
under the title *Lucifer's Daughter*

she acted more tactfully
than a certain Svetlana

2

the note in *The Voice of the Pacific*
is adorned with a photograph
of the deceased

a stout woman
hewn from good wood
stands
against the background of a wall

in one hand
she holds a leather object

something intermediate
between a lady's dressing case
and a mailman's pouch

Mr. Cogito's attention
is riveted
not by Maria's Asiatic face
the small bear's eyes
thickset silhouette of a former dancer
but exactly
by this obstinately held
leather object

what
did she
carry
through wildernesses
deserts of cities
forests
mountains
valleys

    —Petersburg nights
    —a samovar from Tula
    —an Old Church Slavonic hymnal
    —a stolen silver ladle
      with the monogram of the Empress
    —a tooth of Saint Cyril
    —war and peace
    —a wizened pearl in herbs
    —a congealed lump of earth
    —an icon

no one will ever find out
she took the pouch
with her

3

now
the terrestrial remains
of Maria Rasputin
daughter of the last demon
of the last Romanovs
rest in an American cemetery

unmourned
by a Russian kolokol
a patriarch's bass

what is she doing
in this entirely incongruous place
that recalls a picnic
a hilarious weekend of dead stiffs
or the rosy-white crowning finale
of a confectioners' competition

only the boxwood and the birds
speak of eternity

O Maria
—thinks Mr. Cogito
Maria faraway castellan's daughter
with thick red hands

Laura of no one

The Trial

During his great speech the prosecutor
kept piercing me with his yellow index finger
I'm afraid I didn't appear self-assured
unintentionally I put on a mask of fear and depravity
like a rat caught in a trap an informer a fratricide
the reporters were dancing a war dance
slowly I burned at a stake of magnesia

all of this took place in a small stifling room
the floor creaked plaster fell from the ceiling
I counted knots in the boards holes in the wall faces
the faces were alike almost identical
policemen the tribunal witnesses the audience
they belonged to the party of those without any pity
and even my defender smiling pleasantly
was an honorary member of the firing squad

in the first row sat an old fat woman
dressed up as my mother with a theatrical gesture she raised
a handkerchief to her dirty eyes but didn't cry
it must have lasted a long time I don't know even how long
the red blood of the sunset was rising in the gowns of the judges

the real trial went on in my cells
they certainly knew the verdict earlier
after a short rebellion they capitulated and started to die
one after the other
I looked in amazement at my wax fingers

I didn't speak the last word and yet
for so many years I was composing the final speech
to God to the court of the world to the conscience
to the dead rather than the living
roused to my feet by the guards
I managed only to blink and then
the room burst out in healthy laughter

my adoptive mother laughed also
the gavel banged and this really was the end

but what happened after that—death by a noose
or perhaps a punishment generously changed to a dungeon
I'm afraid there is a third dark solution
beyond the limits of time the senses and reason

therefore when I wake I don't open my eyes
I clench my fingers don't lift my head
breathe lightly because truly I don't know
how many minutes of air I still have left

Isadora Duncan

She was not beautiful the nose somewhat ducklike
connoisseurs highly valued the rest of her carnal form
they must be believed but now no one
will recreate her dancing bring Isadora to life
she will remain an enigma in tulle a mystery
like the writing of the Mayas like the Gioconda's smile

She owed her sky-high fame
to what was in bad taste perhaps like Nero's poems
stage moans of the divine Sarah the roars of Holliday
a murderous power is held by the zeitgeist
that is the devil of fashion the devil of passing time
the epoch's clock stops—the gods go down to the bottom

She knew the Greeks as well as an average girl
from the state of Ohio can know them
possessed by a vision of an imaginary Hellas
Bourdelle sculpted her in the form of a bacchante

Lightheartedly she disclosed the secrets of her heart and alcove
in a censurable book with the title "My Life"

Since then we know exactly how the actor Beregy
revealed to her the world of the senses how madly in love
was Gordon Craig Konstantin Stanislavski
hordes of musicians nabobs writers
while Paris Singer threw everything
he had at her feet—an empire
of never-failing sewing machines et cetera

O if Euripides lived at that time
certainly he would have fallen in love with her or hated her
and given her a role in a tragedy for all eternity

The more her talent faded the more feverishly
she believed only dancing can save the world
from misery and suffering this mystical faith

thrust her onto the speaker's platform so she made propaganda
fluids emanated from her as from a great oven
while misery and suffering wouldn't budge like a pillar
clearly she forgot that art hélas cannot save
may Apollo Musagetes pardon her mistake

    Briefly but passionately like everything she did
    she fell in love with the youthful Land of the Soviets and Lenin
    the Star hung on the neck of the Engineer of History

    Unfortunately no spark came from it
    Isadora bored even Heavy Industry and Agriculture
    a revolution in light dancing hops is and was a dream

    The poor thing mistook utopia for truth
    passons since later she was followed by crowds
    of luminaries of learning pastors and Sartres

    Unfortunately she had to bid farewell to the Land of Hope
    as consolation she took a costly poet with her
    the half-conscious Esenin cursed loved howled

        The play's finale was truly worthy of tragedy
        after a life full of flights and falls
        the instrument of death was a cashmere shawl

        too long surely like the tail of a comet
        entangled in the spokes of a car the cashmere shawl
        strangled her like Othello wild with jealousy

And still she dances she is over a hundred years old
a gray old lady pale almost invisible
between greatness and ridiculousness she dances
no longer as ecstatically as before years ago
with the deliberateness of a prioress with mature reflection
she places her naked feet over the abyss

The Messenger

The messenger awaited a desperately long time
the longed-for herald of victory or annihilation
was delayed—the tragedy was without any ending

In the background the chorus scanned dark prophecies and curses
the king—a dynastic fish—thrashed in an inconceivable net
the second indispensable person was absent—fate

The epilogue was probably known by an eagle an oak the wind a sea wave
the spectators were half-dead breathing shallowly as stone
The gods slept A quiet night without lightning

Finally the messenger arrived in a mask of blood of dirt lamentation
uttering incomprehensible shrieks pointing with his hand to the East
this was worse than death because there would be no pity no fear at all
and in the last moment everyone longs to be pardoned

September 17

for Józef Chapski

My defenseless country will admit you invader
where Jaś and little Mary went walking to school
the path won't be split into an abyss

Rivers are too lazy not quick to flood
knights sleeping in the mountains continue to sleep
so you will enter easily uninvited guest

> But sons of the earth will gather at night
> funny *carbonari* plotters of freedom
> they will clean old-fashioned weapons
> will swear on a bird on two colors
>
> And then as always—glows and explosions
> boys like children sleepless commanders
> knapsacks filled with defeat crimson fields of glory
> the strengthening knowledge—we are alone

My defenseless country will admit you invader
and give you a plot of earth under a willow—and peace
so those who come after us will learn again
the most difficult art—the forgiveness of sins

Mr. Cogito on the Need for Precision

1

Mr. Cogito
is alarmed by a problem
in the domain of applied mathematics

the difficulties we encounter
with operations of simple arithmetic

children are lucky
they add apple to apple
subtract grain from grain
the sum is correct
the kindergarten of the world
pulsates with a safe warmth

particles of matter have been measured
heavenly bodies weighed
and only in human affairs
inexcusable carelessness reigns supreme
the lack of precise information

over the immensity of history
wheels a specter
the specter of indefiniteness

how many Greeks were killed at Troy
—we don't know

to give the exact casualties
on both sides
in the battle at Gaugamela
at Agincourt
Leipzig
Kutno

and also the number of victims
of terror
of the white
the red
the brown
—O colors innocent colors—

—we don't know
truly we don't know

Mr. Cogito
rejects the sensible explanation
that this was long ago
the wind has thoroughly mixed the ashes
the blood flowed to the sea

sensible explanations
intensify the alarm
of Mr. Cogito

because even what
is happening under our eyes
evades numbers
loses the human dimension

somewhere there must be an error
a fatal defect in our tools
or a sin of memory

2

a few simple examples
from the accounting of victims

in an airplane disaster
it is easy to establish
the exact number of the dead

important for heirs
and those plunged in grief
for insurance companies

we take the list of passengers
and the crew
next to each name
we place a little cross

it is slightly harder
in the case
of train accidents

bodies torn to pieces
have to be put back together
so no head
remains ownerless

during elemental
catastrophes
the arithmetic
becomes complicated

we count those who are saved
but the unknown remainder
neither alive
nor definitely dead
is described by a strange term
the missing

they still have the chance
to return to us
from fire
from water
the interior of the earth

if they return—that's fine
if they don't—too bad

3

now Mr. Cogito
climbs
to the highest tottering
step of indefiniteness

    how difficult it is to establish the names
    of all those who perished
    in the struggle with inhuman power

    the official statistics
    reduce their number
    once again pitilessly
    they decimate those who have died a violent death
    and their bodies disappear
    in abysmal cellars
    of huge police buildings

    eyewitnesses
    blinded by gas
    deafened by salvoes
    by fear and despair
    are inclined toward exaggeration

    accidental observers
    give doubtful figures
    accompanied by the shameful
    word "about"

    and yet in these matters
    accuracy is essential
    we must not be wrong
    even by a single one

    we are despite everything
    the guardians of our brothers

    ignorance about those who have disappeared
    undermines the reality of the world

it thrusts into the hell of appearances
the devilish net of dialectics
proclaiming there is no difference
between the substance and the specter

    therefore we have to know
    to count exactly
    call by the first name
    provide for a journey

    in a bowl of clay
    millet poppy seeds
    a bone comb
    arrowheads
    and a ring of faithfulness

    amulets

The Power of Taste

for Professor Izydora Dambska

It didn't require great character at all
our refusal disagreement and resistance
we had a shred of necessary courage
but fundamentally it was a matter of taste
                              Yes taste
in which there are fibers of soul the cartilage of conscience

Who knows if we had been better and more attractively tempted
sent rose-skinned women thin as a wafer
or fantastic creatures from the paintings of Hieronymus Bosch
but what kind of hell was there at this time
a wet pit the murderers' alley the barrack
called a palace of justice
a home-brewed Mephisto in a Lenin jacket
sent Aurora's grandchildren out into the field
boys with potato faces
very ugly girls with red hands

Verily their rhetoric was made of cheap sacking
(Marcus Tullius kept turning in his grave)
chains of tautologies a couple of concepts like flails
the dialectics of slaughterers no distinctions in reasoning
syntax deprived of beauty of the subjunctive

So aesthetics can be helpful in life
one should not neglect the study of beauty

Before we declare our consent we must carefully examine
the shape of the architecture the rhythm of the drums and pipes
official colors the despicable ritual of funerals

          Our eyes and ears refused obedience
          the princes of our senses proudly chose exile

It did not require great character at all
we had a shred of necessary courage

[69

but fundamentally it was a matter of taste
                              Yes taste
that commands us to get out to make a wry face draw out a sneer
even if for this the precious capital of the body the head
                                        must fall

Mr. Cogito—
Notes from the House of the Dead

1

we lay in a row
in the depths of the temple of the absurd
anointed with suffering
in a wet shroud of terror

like fruit
fallen
from the tree of life
rotting separately
each in its own way
only in this a remnant
of humanity lay dormant

by an inconceivable verdict
stripped of the throne of the primates
resembling coelenterates
protozoa
hookworms

deprived
of ambition
of existence

       and then
       at ten o'clock in the evening
       when the lights were turned out
       unexpectedly
       like all revelations
       spoke
       a voice

       masculine
       slow

commanding
the rising
of the dead

a voice
powerful
majestic
leading
from the house of slavery

we lay side by side
low
listening with rapt attention

as it
rose
above us

2

no one knew
his face

tightly locked
in an inaccessible place
called
debir
in the very heart
of the treasury

under the guard of cruel priests
under the guard of cruel angels

we called him Adam
meaning taken from the earth

at ten in the evening
when the lights were switched off
Adam would begin his concert

to the ears of the profane
it sounded
like the howl of a person in fetters

for us
an epiphany

he was
anointed
the sacrificial animal
author of psalms

he sang
the inconceivable desert
the call of the abyss
the noose on the heights

Adam's cry
was made
of two or three vowels
stretched out like ribs on the horizon

then
suddenly
a break

the tearing of space

and again
like nearby thunder
the same two three
vowels

an avalanche of rocks
voice of many waters
trumpets of judgment

and there was
no complaint in it

or request
not even a shadow of dolor

he grew
became powerful
staggering

a dark column
pushing aside
the stars

3

after a few concerts
he fell silent

the illumination of his voice
lasted a brief time

he didn't redeem
his followers

they took Adam away
or he retreated
into eternity

the source
of the rebellion
was extinguished

      and perhaps
      only I
      still hear
      the echo
      of his voice

      more and more slender
      quieter
      further and further away

like music of the spheres
the harmony of the universe

so perfect
it is inaudible

Report from the Besieged City

Too old to carry arms and fight like the others—

they graciously gave me the inferior role of chronicler
I record—I don't know for whom—the history of the siege

I am supposed to be exact but I don't know when the invasion began
two hundred years ago in December in September perhaps yesterday at
    dawn
everyone here suffers from a loss of the sense of time

all we have left is the place the attachment to the place
we still rule over the ruins of temples specters of gardens and houses
if we lose the ruins nothing will be left

I write as I can in the rhythm of interminable weeks
monday: empty storehouses a rat became the unit of currency
tuesday: the mayor murdered by unknown assailants
wednesday: negotiations for a cease-fire the enemy has imprisoned our
    messengers
we don't know where they are held that is the place of torture
thursday: after a stormy meeting a majority of voices rejected
the motion of the spice merchants for unconditional surrender
friday: the beginning of the plague saturday: our invincible defender
N.N. committed suicide sunday: no more water we drove back
an attack at the eastern gate called the Gate of the Alliance

all of this is monotonous I know it can't move anyone

I avoid any commentary I keep a tight hold on my emotions I write about
    the facts
only they it seems are appreciated in foreign markets
yet with a certain pride I would like to inform the world
that thanks to the war we have raised a new species of children
our children don't like fairy tales they play at killing

awake and asleep they dream of soup of bread and bones
just like dogs and cats

in the evening I like to wander near the outposts of the City
along the frontier of our uncertain freedom
I look at the swarms of soldiers below their lights
I listen to the noise of drums barbarian shrieks
truly it is inconceivable the City is still defending itself
the siege has lasted a long time the enemies must take turns
nothing unites them except the desire for our extermination
Goths the Tartars Swedes troops of the Emperor regiments of the
        Transfiguration
who can count them
the colors of their banners change like the forest on the horizon
from delicate bird's yellow in spring through green through red to
        winter's black

and so in the evening released from facts I can think
about distant ancient matters for example our
friends beyond the sea I know they sincerely sympathize
they send us flour lard sacks of comfort and good advice
they don't even know their fathers betrayed us
our former allies at the time of the second Apocalypse
their sons are blameless they deserve our gratitude therefore we are
        grateful
they have not experienced a siege as long as eternity
those struck by misfortune are always alone
the defenders of the Dalai Lama the Kurds the Afghan mountaineers

now as I write these words the advocates of conciliation
have won the upper hand over the party of inflexibles
a normal hesitation of moods fate still hangs in the balance

cemeteries grow larger the number of defenders is smaller
yet the defense continues it will continue to the end
and if the City falls but a single man escapes
he will carry the City within himself on the roads of exile
he will be the City

we look in the face of hunger the face of fire face of death
worst of all—the face of betrayal

and only our dreams have not been humiliated

(1982)

Translators' Notes

What I Saw   The original version of this poem was published in *Morze i Ziemia* (Gdańsk) in 1957. The censors did not permit the poem to be published in book form.

From the Top of the Stairs   This poem was written shortly after the workers' revolt in Poznań in 1956, and was published the following year in the periodical *Po Prostu*. The censors did not permit this poem, either, to be included in one of Herbert's collections of poems.

Mr. Cogito's Soul   The persona "Mr. Cogito" first made his appearance in Herbert's fifth collection of poems, entitled *Pan Cogito* (*Mr. Cogito*, 1974). The use of this persona carries over from the 1974 volume. The "soul" of Mr. Cogito is feminine largely because the Polish word for soul is of feminine gender.

Mr. Cogito—the Return   In the Polish original "How are you" is in English.

Mr. Cogito and the Imagination   "The piano at the top of the Alps" approximates a phrase in Rimbaud's *Illuminations* (in "Après le Déluge").

In Memoriam Nagy László   The Hungarian poet László Nagy (1925–1978) was a member of the same generation as Herbert, and like Herbert he studied the fine arts before becoming a poet.

To Ryszard Krynicki—a Letter   Ryszard Krynicki (1943–   ), a younger Polish poet and member of the "Nowa Fala" or New Wave of poets that became active in the late 1960s and 1970s. After publishing two volumes in Poland, Krynicki was officially banned from publication there in 1977. The "garden of betrayal": the word *ogrójec* also connotes the Garden of Olives, Gethsemane.

Photograph   The river Hipanis or Hypanis is now the southern Bug.

Babylon   The "portrait of a young lady" by Petrus Christus hangs in the Dahlem Museum in West Berlin.

The Murderers of Kings   Herbert has said that "Regis" was an Austrian physician and author of a book about "great men" from the point of view of medicine. François Ravaillac (1578–1610) was a schoolmaster and former monk who assassinated the French King Henri IV. Gavrilo Princip (1895–1918) assassinated the Archduke Francis Ferdinand and his wife at Sarajevo in 1914. Jacques Clément (1567–1589) was a French Dominican monk who assassinated Henri III of France. Sante Ieronimo Caserio (1873–1894), an Italian anarchist, stabbed to death Sadi Carnot, the president of the French Republic.

September 17   September 17, 1939, was the date of the attack on Eastern Poland by the Red Army when the Soviet Union was allied with Nazi Germany. The *carbonari* were a secret political association organized in Italy in the nineteenth century to establish a republic.

Mr. Cogito on the Need for Precision   The battle of Gaugamela took place in 331 B.C. near Nineveh in Assyria.

The Power of Taste   "flails": the Polish word that means literally "flail"—*cep*—has also the colloquial meaning of "idiot."

Mr. Cogito—Notes from the House of the Dead   "debir": a Hebrew word meaning a sanctuary or innermost room of a temple.

Report from the Besieged City "Two hundred years ago": between 1772 and 1795 Poland was partitioned three times by Prussia, Russia, and Austria. The Third Partition lasted until the end of World War I. "December": General Jaruzelski siezed power, declaring a "state of war," on December 13, 1981. "September": the attacks on Poland by both Hitler and Stalin occurred in September. "regiments of the Transfiguration": the Preobrazhenskii Regiment, one of the first of the Russian regular standing army, was formed by the tsar Peter in 1699.